Marry me, Memorably!

An Ultimate Guide to Craft WOW WEDDINGS
Celebrating Love, Luxury & Life

Vikrant Kuthiala

The Unforgettable Wedding Expert

Vikrant Kuthiala

The Unforgettable Wedding Expert

Worldwide Published by

Pendown Press

PENDOWN PRESS LLP
An ISO 9001 & ISO 14001 Certified Co.,
Regd. Office: 3767A, Kanhaiya Nagar,
Tri Nagar, Delhi-110035
Ph.: 8130886000, 9650072927, 8595249536
E-mail: info@pendownpress.com
Branch Office: 1A/2A, 20, Hari Sadan, Ansari Road,
Daryaganj, New Delhi-110002
Ph.: 011-45794768
Website: PendownPress.com

First Edition: 2023
Price: ₹399/-
ISBN: 978-93-5554-700-2

Layout and Cover Designed by Pendown Graphics Team
Printed and Bound in India by Thomson Press India Ltd.

Gratitude

I express my deepest gratitude to my **Guru & Mentor Akshar Yadav.**

The word Guru is made up of two words 'Gu' which means ignorance and 'Ru' which means the destroyer.

A Guru is one who destroys your ignorance, makes you look at yourself in the mirror, makes you introspect, grinds you, motivates you, polishes you and leads you from darkness to light.

AY is all that and so much more.

I am truly blessed by divine providence to be brought into his universe.

Thank You, AY

Foreword

Your Wedding Day is a unique moment in time that celebrates the unbreakable bond between you and your betrothed. The love you have found is unique and beautiful and your wedding should reflect who you both are. Making your wedding memorable and not a run-of-the-mill celebration is the desire of all couples.

If you want your wedding to be remembered for years to come, doing it all on your own can prove to be challenging. You need an expert, a visionary, a creative experienced observer, and a passionate person to guide, plan & execute everything to perfection.

If you are reading this then you are fortunate enough to have found one- It is none other than the author of this book!

Vikrant Kuthiala is a widely travelled person whose keen sense of observation, first-hand feel of social events, and intense desire to improve events, in particular weddings has made him an expert in his own right.

He is a man with bright ideas and can guide and educate you with a   complete sense of responsibility from the designing & printing of invitation cards to the preparation of excellent cuisines.

He is so much more than a wedding planner or a wedding designer; he is the Unforgettable Wedding Expert.

In, this book for the first time he shares with his readers excellent ideas about organising weddings and how they can curate memorable weddings that will amaze every invitee, leaving them with unforgettable memories for years to come.

This book will indeed prove to be a boon for all who are looking to create wedding memories.

I wish him the very best with this book.

Zaffar Shah
Senior Advocate

Dedication

This book is dedicated to my soulmate Aparna, who has stood with me through thick and thin, through all the rides on the roller coaster that is life. I would not be what I am today without her love and care.

To my son Shreyas and my daughter Ananya for all the joy, love & care they have given me throughout my life.

To my Parents, Siblings and In-laws, each one has guided me, moulded me and handheld me on my journey.

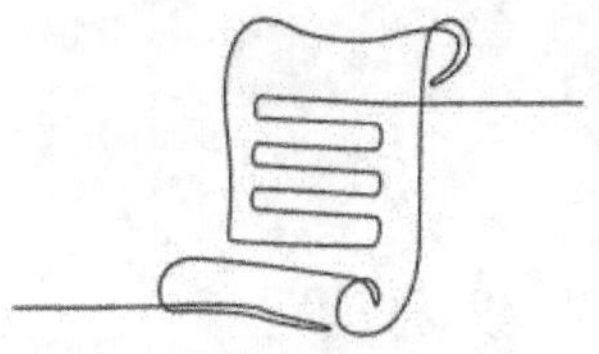

Contents

Chapter 1

HELLO! LET'S GET ACQUAINTED

Hello, I am Vikrant Kuthiala. I live in the beautiful and holy City of Jammu, nestled in the foothills of the Himalayas, in the Union Territory of Jammu & Kashmir. Jammu is also well known as the City of Temples.

Coming from a business family, I am a 4th Generation Entrepreneur. The family from the early 1930s was in the business of Timber. I joined the business actively in 1980 when I independently managed the installation of the Main Wooden Flooring at the Indira Gandhi Indraprastha Indoor Stadium at Raj Ghat, Delhi, for the 1982 Asian Games.

In addition to the family timber business, with entrepreneurial blood flowing fiercely in my veins, I have ventured into & succeeded in varied sectors. I have been a Steel Producer running Mini Steel Plants located in Faridabad, New Delhi and Jammu, operated an Arc Furnace, Induction Furnace and Ladle Refining Furnace, a Billet Casting Machine and a CTD/TMT Steel Bars Rolling Mill from 1982 to 2013.

In 2016, I established a Modern Cash and Carry Best Price Walmart Store in Jammu, which is now operated by Flipkart.

Finally, since 2016, I have been managing Vedas, A preferred destination for memorable weddings and functions located in scenic Jammu.

I have always been active in working for the upliftment of entrepreneurs and businesses, and to this end, I have served as

Chairman and member of various industry federations such as the Chamber of Commerce and Industry, the Jammu Regional Committee of the PHD Chamber of Commerce and Industry, New Delhi, J&K State Committee of Federation of Industries (FII), Regional Advisory Committee of Central Excise & Customs, the Board of The J&K Bank Limited etc.

And continue to serve in various capacities in various organizations as

Chamber of Commerce & Industry, Jammu, the J&K State Regional Branch of the Indian Institute of Public Administration (IIPA) Honorary Treasurer, Sh. Ramakrishna Mission, Jammu Mangaing Committee Member, President Jammu Chapter of the Mayo College Alumni Association.

Childhood Desire Turns into Purpose

As a family-oriented person, relationships and bonding have always been extremely important to me. Even as a child, I would be overjoyed when the whole family would gather together for functions, ceremonies or vacations.

As a child, even though I was carefree and joyful during these occasions, being sensitive, I also noticed that the adults in charge of the arrangements would often appear flustered and agitated instead of being happy and enjoying the occasion unconditionally.

Later, of course, as an adult, from my own experience and observing others, I did learn that being in charge of a function/party/event/occasion is a full-time, high-pressure, unpaid job that robs you of the pleasure of letting go and enjoying and making memories fully.

Think of a wedding if you are the parent— Tell me, were you able to dance freely when your daughter pulled you onto the dance floor lovingly? Your mind was running through the long list of unfinished arrangements to be supervised— the lights, the flowers, the caterers, and the list is endless.

I always wished I could take that burden off their shoulders and help everyone enjoy occasions with friends and family and make memories for a lifetime, especially for weddings.

A wedding, whether it's your own that you are planning (as a lot of young couples do today) or your children's— your joy knows no bounds, and you deserve to enjoy and memorize every moment without a care in the world.

For the past many years with Vedas— A preferred destination for weddings (and other events), I have been able to gift people carefree, well-planned & executed, joyous weddings that they will treasure as memories for years to come.

I am on a mission to help parents (and anyone else planning a wedding) organize Weddings smoothly and generate a lifetime of memories full of joy, love, laughter, and undiluted happiness.

And further in this book, I will show you exactly how to do that!

And now that I have introduced myself to you— It's your turn. Well, well, well— Here's the surprise— I have already made an effort to get to know you, and I know you.

You are a wonderful, beautiful human being looking forward to one of the most important events of your life, and you are committed to making it the best ever without stressing yourself out, but lately, you have begun to believe that perhaps it may not be possible. Often you find yourself wishing that there was a magic wand you could wave and make your/your child's wedding perfect yet stress-free.

Dear reader, don't give up hope; you are holding that magic wand in your hand right now!

Yes! This book is your portal to having the magical, fairytale wedding (or a minimalist one if you so choose) of your dreams completely stress-free.

Let me show you how..............

THE SILVER LINING BEHIND
THE CLOUDS

Every Challenge is a Gift- A Book is Born

The two years of COVID-19 were a dark, ominous cloud that shrouded the world in uncertainty and losses. While every sector was hit hard, certain sectors were hit even harder such as hospitality.

These years were extremely tough for the Hospitality and Banqueting/Event Industry in specific, with forced shutdowns and restrictions on the number of guests on one side and the need to sustain the organisation in meeting legal requirements and ensuring payment of salaries to staff and workers- the future looked extremely bleak. However, this forced me to look at the whole business from different angles.

Hard times call for hard measures, and to sustain ourselves during this period, we were forced to look at all the scenarios and ultimately had to deploy several cost-cutting measures, defer some payments, and look at alternate revenue streams to survive.

One of the unique & innovative decisions we made at this time was to start a Cloud Kitchen by leveraging cyber technology as a separate business to keep our kitchen operational and staff occupied and add a separate vertical to generate revenue.

What I also found out during this period was that most of the guests who hosted functions had no idea as to what went into curating a memorable function.

They had only vague ideas on how to organise a marriage effectively. For most of the guests, everything was in the form of a mental chart, from where they were operating under a constant state of pressure and somehow trying to meet deadlines, and, more often than not, settling for less than the best.

Having seen these struggles closely yet objectively from the other side, I felt compelled to help everyone to organise memorable weddings minus the stress overload. While pondering on ways to do the same, it struck me that writing a concise, focused guidebook/ handbook on organising memorable weddings stress-free was the perfect way to reach the maximum number of people and impact their lives positively.

To be truly honest, in order to organize a memorable wedding, any family has to organize and manage over 100 separate but inter-independent activities.

However, to keep this book highly focused and on-point, I am sharing with you the most critical aspects only, but hey, don't worry— I will write in detail about the other activities, too, in subsequent books.

The reason people, including my clients, peers, colleagues, vendors and associates, find me credible is because

Rated 5 Stars for Hygiene

Zomato Rating 4.1 Stars

The Dynamics of Change in the Event Industry

The current scenario in my industry is one of change & uncertainty due to changing family dynamics with the added pressure of aspirational goals due to the advent of social media and also in the mix is the problem of plenty— Clients have too many choices and are confused about making the right choice..........

Earlier, the family structure used to be a joint family and everyone in the extended family would chip in and help in organizing the festivities. Now, most families are nuclear with one or two children. The support from extended family, friends and relatives is extremely limited in most cases.

On the other end, the choice of service providers with the venues, catering companies, event managers, and decorators are infinite, with each claiming to be better than the best. The hosts, in most cases, are thoroughly confused and have no objective means to make rational decisions.

Given this situation, hosts do not get the full value for their money and end up with less-than-ideal events due to a series of wrong decisions.

What This Book Will Give You

Having worked extensively in this space over the past few years, **I have identified a series of factors which, if handled properly, will lead to a tension-free cost-effective wedding function.**

And I promise you that if you follow the sequence and the strategies and take the precautions highlighted, not only will you save a substantial amount of money, but you will have a wedding without stress and tension.

By **not reading this book** and missing out on the strategies and actions highlighted in this book, **you are sure to spend much more time and money than you should in hosting a wedding** additionally, you will, in all probability, **end up with tension and stress;** you will be firefighting from one crisis to another crisis and have a wedding memorable for all the wrong reasons.

I am on a mission to help parents organize weddings smoothly and generate a lifetime of memories full of joy, love, laughter, and undiluted happiness.

So, let us deep dive. I want you to recognize the opportunity which is in your hands to become a wedding planning expert, use this book to organize your wedding in an easy and stress-free manner. I am confident that much could come from such a powerful tool, and you will definitely have a Wedding which people will talk about and recall for a long, long time.

Chapter 3

MISSION: PERFECT-PICTURESQUE-PEACEFUL WEDDINGS

As shared earlier, my vision and mission are to help and guide parents/anyone hosting a wedding to host memorable weddings and generate a lifetime of memories which your family and friends will cherish and recall for decades thereafter.

When I see people (usually parents, but even the bride & groom in new-age couples) stuck and struggling to put wedding events together, it saddens me, and I wish to remedy that through this book.

I have previously helped organize 665+ functions, and now I share this knowledge with you so that you can benefit from it and pass it on further to others who, too, could be benefitted.

I am writing this book to share my knowledge and expertise far and wide for the benefit of everyone seeking the perfect wedding...

And before we move on to the transformative practical content, I would like to acknowledge and thank all the people who have worked with me through various phases of my life, told me why they chose to work with me, gave feedback and encouraged me when I slipped and supported me with priceless advice and suggestions. I would not be half the person without my team and my vendors & associates. Thank you for being a part of this glorious journey and helping make people's wedding dreams come true. And immense gratitude to my clients for trusting me with your most important day and for recommending us further wholeheartedly.

I would also appreciate it if all of you, my readers, share your feedback/inputs on the link provided at the end of the book. Your opinion and suggestions are precious.

Having worked with 665+ clients, I have identified the main pain areas, the patterns, the pitfalls, and the corrective steps which you need to take at each stage. Most of us would, at some level or the other, be aware of these aspects. This book will remind you of those and shed light on some more areas and help you recall those which you may have forgotten or ignored.

Chapter 4

THE INDIAN WEDDING LANDSCAPE

Before we get into the pro tips & techniques of organizing a memorable wedding, let's first acquaint ourselves and familiarize ourselves with the wedding event landscape.

The Magical Service Components

To learn and perfect the Art of Memorable Weddings, it is imperative to understand what comprises the wedding industry.

So what exactly makes up the wedding industry?

Here's all you need to know

The Wedding Industry includes:

- Event Venues
- Caterers
- Decorators
- Florists
- Event Managers
- Jewellers
- Beauticians
- Hair & Makeup artists
- Gift Packaging
- Designers for Trousseau

- ➤ Tailors & Drapers
- ➤ Clothing Accesssiorisers
- ➤ Choreographers
- ➤ VideoGraphers
- ➤ Photographers
- ➤ DJ's
- ➤ Singers & Performers
- ➤ Printers
- ➤ Bar Tenders
- ➤ Valets
- ➤ Travel Agencies
- ➤ Fireworks & Pyros
- ➤ Event Destinations
- ➤ Hotels
- ➤ Transport Service Providers
- ➤ Security Services.

The list could be longer, of course, but these are the ones you need to focus on.

Money Matters

Budget and expense management is the key to controlling stress and making a wedding memorable. Therefore know what to spend where— to do this, you need to be acquainted with the financial landscape of weddings.

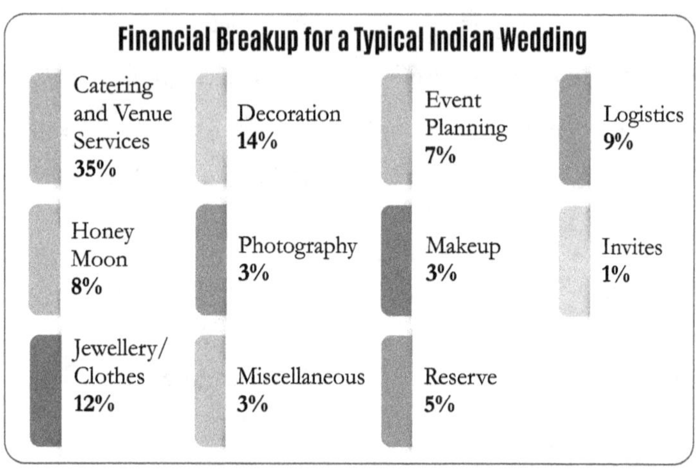

Some Facts to Ponder

Some Facts to Ponder

- Half of the Indian population is under 29 years of age.
- The Wedding Industry is heading for a boom this decade.
- The current size of the Indian wedding industry is 3.68 Lakh crores.

*[*Source: Forbes India, Dec 2022]*

- The Annual Growth Rate of this industry is projected to be 25% to 30 %.
- In 2022, 3.2 Million Wedding Events were held in India.

*[*Source: Money Control, Nov 23rd, 2022]*

Given this huge young population, the wedding industry is slated to grow in an unprecedented manner. As a result, the cost of all wedding services is slated to go up dramatically over the next few years.

This makes it imperative that all aspects of a wedding are properly planned and budgeted for.

There is nothing more important than this.

■ ■ ■ ■

Chapter 5

WEDDING BASICS

When we say the word wedding, it generally conjures up an image of grandeur, pageantry, festivities and celebration.

A wedding is an event to celebrate togetherness with family and friends, over feasts and generate unlimited joy all around.

At the heart of it all, a wedding needs the following:

1. A Groom.

2. A Bride.

3. A Priest, Father, Maulvi or any other relevant religious officiant to perform the ceremony & rituals.

4. Registry- someone to make it official.

Given these 4, weddings can be solemnized.

So let's begin the memorable wedding planning journey from the time the couple gets engaged—

Post Engagement

Now that the couple is engaged, you have to plan and finalize the following components of your wedding. Follow the checklist sequence shared here, and you will sail through your perfect wedding with no sweat.

Let's begin the flow— the first 5 things you need to decide on are:

1. The Wedding Date.
2. What functions do you plan to hold?
3. Will the functions be held in the same city or in multiple cities?
4. The Guest List.
5. The Venues for each function.

Essentially, the answer to these 5 will determine the choices to be made.

However, before deciding on anything, the Bride, Groom and their families need to:

Decide on the kind of wedding they want I.E:

1. A community celebration.
2. An intimate wedding.
3. A wedding limited to friends.
4. An Over-the-top Wedding.
5. A Destination Wedding.

All your decisions, however, should be rooted in this -

> Always remember, what **your guests will remember are the emotions** that are, the care you took of them by giving them **good food, a visually Aesthetic Decor, the Service, and the Venue** provided to your guests (care).
>
> Everyone remembers how a function felt, how the food tasted, how it looked, and how much they were cared for.

You have to be clear on what you want your wedding to look like -

- ➢ Modern
- ➢ Traditional
- ➢ Subtle & Lowkey- Minimalistic
- ➢ Extravagant

Once you have decided on all these parameters, it's time to proceed to make the wedding lists..

■ ■ ■ ■

Chapter 6

CHECK IT OFF- THE POWER OF LISTS

Now that the engagement is finalized, it is time for the wedding list to be worked on, as all consequent selections will be based on the list.

The first thing to do is figure out

The Guest List:

A. The Grooms List.

B. The Brides List.

It is important that Individual guest lists be made for both the families for all the functions separately...

Out of these lists, there would be some invitees from both sides who will be invited for all the functions, this will form the **"Core List"**.

Lists should be prioritized on the basis of:

1. Must be invited.

2. Likely to be invited.

3. May be invited.

4. Not to be invited.

Note: Your lists will need to be reviewed periodically as you start factoring in venue selection/availability, cost and other things.

**A guest list may increase or decrease.*

Tips for Making a Guest List

Making a guest list is by no means an easy task— It's a big event, your joy overflows and you want everyone to be a part of it, but of course, there are limitations. Who to invite and who to leave out can be the biggest stressors indeed. Here's how to go about it systematically and smoothly to fine-comb your list.

Go one by one through -

➢ Family

➢ Friends

➢ Classmates

➢ Relatives/Extended family

➢ Neighbours

➢ Business Associates

➢ Doctors, Engineers, Architects, CA's (Professionals) you are associated with

➢ Acquaintances

Then you need to work out:

➢ Are you planning to invite Children?

➢ Are you permitting Singles to get someone with them?

➢ Have you accounted for uninvited friends, neighbours, and uninvited guests turning up?

➢ How many guests are local?

➢ How many are from out of town?

Memorable Wedding PROTIP

Invite people you love and who love you in return— (avoid tension generators)

Get the venue to curate the wedding around your guest list.

For example, if the guest list consists of elderly people, additional seating, soft music, and extensive table service need to be provided.

If your guest list consists of youngsters, elaborate DJ setups and additional Bar Tenders may be required.

If it is a mixed list, then the arrangements need to be moderated accordingly.

You have to see who is coming and book the venue so as to meet that requirement

To keep things smooth and memorable, you must ensure the following:

➢ The guests must be made aware of what to expect, as in the case of winter, if functions are in the open, guests must be informed to come adequately clad.

> ➤ Make sure, your guests feel cared for at every stage— You will need to fine-tune with the venue and service providers.

> ➤ Always feed your guests on time. Hungry guests are never happy guests.

■ ■ ■ ■

Chapter 7

MANAGING THE WEDDING FINANCIALS

More often than not, the biggest source of stress, apart from people not sticking to timelines, can be your budget.

Right at the outset, be clear as to the amount of money you want to spend on the wedding/functions. Don't just randomly keep choosing products and services and paying for them.

After you've set up an umbrella budget, apportion the amount under the following heads:

Checklist- a Link to a dynamic checklist is provided at the end of this book with a QR code

Decide the number/list of your functions as per the example below (* this, of course, may be different for everyone, so please personalize this list as per your choices.)

➢ **Function 1:** Wedding/Barat.

➢ **Function 2:** Mehndi Raat.

➢ **Function 3:** Cocktail.

➢ **Function 4:** Reception

Expenditure Head

➢ Venue charges	➢ Food (catering) charges
➢ Decor charges	➢ DJ
➢ Singers/Performers	➢ Photographer/ Videographer.
➢ Beauticians, Groomers, Makeup Artists	➢ Bar License
➢ Bartender	➢ Alcohol
➢ Valets	➢ Band
➢ Pony	➢ Jewelry
➢ Clothing	➢ Brides/Grooms Attire- other likely costs
➢ Hotel Bookings	➢ Taxis/Transport
➢ Honey Moon	➢ Miscellaneous

Strategic Reserve

Typically 5 to 7 % over and above your planned budget should always be kept aside for unforeseen expenses.

Sometimes the difference between a very good and an exceptional wedding is a little more money spent on a better venue, food and décor.

Once you calculate the budget, based on your price bands, for each head, you then have to identify the best fit for each category.

Your guest list would have to be adjusted based on your financial planning and selection of venue.

You will have to prioritize what is most important to you, eg., the food, décor, the DJ, the personal care, the proximity of the venue, whatever it may be, you will have to prioritize and spend accordingly.

Depending on the price bands and your priorities, your budget may need adjustment from one head to another, which you must ensure that you carry out internally before committing to anyone.

You will need to be really clear on your budget as, beyond a point, it would be very difficult to cut down the number of guests, as these would be core invitees.

Once your guest list is completed, you will have to assess it critically.

How many guests are likely to turn up?

My experience is that in most cases, 80-85% of the confirmed guests turn up. You need to make an assessment and take an informed guess from the firm arrivals and book accordingly.

Instead of confirming all Hotel bookings, see if it is possible to keep some rooms on a standby basis.

Memorable Wedding PROTIP 1

Your wedding financial planning and your guest list will determine all your decisions. The venue you select, the food you serve, the kind of décor you choose, and so on and so forth.

Memorable Wedding PROTIP 2

Always work with your NUMBERS!

Assess, reassess and re-reassess your numbers, first and foremost and then plan and work on everything else.

Your guests are an important component of your wedding. Their care is the primary consideration, based on this number, you must work out everything else.

Always, invite everyone who you want to be a part of your wedding, never ever restrict this list.

Anyone, who you are indifferent to and do not want to invite, limit them.

Once you have carried out the exercises shared in the previous chapter and finalized your guest list, and worked out your numbers, see if you are ok with it.

Do you have the scope to increase the numbers?

Do you need to decrease the numbers?

***LATE INVITATIONS, which feel like an afterthought, can be counterproductive, so be very very careful in sending out late invitations.**

Create a Guest List Spreadsheet with the QR

I have created a guest list spreadsheet, especially for you.

The spreadsheet must incorporate:

- ➢ Name
- ➢ Sur Name
- ➢ Title
- ➢ Address
- ➢ Primary Mobile
- ➢ Secondary Mobile
- ➢ e-mail
- ➢ The Serial number of the invitee,
- ➢ RSVP/Card/
- ➢ Link/attendance
- ➢ Criteria for Attendance
- ➢ Age
- ➢ Fitness
- ➢ Place of residence
- ➢ Clash with other functions, hosted by someone else
- ➢ Function(s) each guest is invited to.

Now that you have finalized your guest list and financial outlay, you need to book your Venue at the earliest.

Chapter 8

THE HEART OF THE WEDDING
THE VENUE

As you are all aware, Indian wedding dates tend to be limited to a few dates in a year and good venues, caterers, and professionals tend to get booked early, which limits your choices to less than best.

If you are not proactive, you will have to settle for less than ideal.

In the following chapters, I will highlight some crucial aspects which you must assess to identify the right and professional service providers. Let's begin with the heart -center — **the venue.**

Event Venues

There are multiple options for booking event venues & I am sharing them with their pros & cons below, so you can make an informed choice best suited to your needs.

A. Outright Rental

In this scenario, you just get the use of the venue & you will need to arrange your own caterer, own Decor and also arrange a host of other service providers as per your choice & requirements.

Typically, such venues charge a fixed amount of rent, and they provide a fixed number of waiters with basic tableware and basic décor (more or less, the same decor will exist throughout the season).

The Pros:

- You have a wide variety to choose from as they come in all shapes and sizes.

- Also, you may be able to negotiate better prices in this kind of a deal.

The Cons:

- They are not bothered about the quality of food or decor, as the price is the only criterion, and if anything goes wrong, they have only rented the premises; beyond that, there is no responsibility.

***GST on the rental is currently 18%.**

B. Hotels

Then, of course, another popular form of venue is hotels where the wedding or related events can be hosted either in a hotel ballroom, a lawn or both.

Pros:

- By choosing a hotel, the host is likely to get an added status boost of hosting functions at a prominent hotel. (though this is purely a social and psychological benefit and not a practical, organizational or financial one))

- Logistically this is a great choice as the guests can stay in the hotel itself, and no extra transportation to and from the function venue will be required.

Cons:

The cons, though, are quite a few, so be careful and think hard before choosing this option.

1. **Cost:** One of the biggest disadvantages of having a wedding function in a hotel is the cost. Hotels can be expensive, and you may end up paying a premium for the venue, catering, and other services.

2. **Limited customization:** Most hotels have strict policies and guidelines for their events, which can limit your ability to customize the wedding to your liking.

3. **Availability:** Depending on the time of the year and the location, hotels may not have availability on your desired wedding date.

4. **Décor restrictions:** Many hotels have strict policies on decorating, which can limit your ability to create the ambience and atmosphere you want.

5. **Crowd management:** Hotels can be crowded, especially during peak season. This can create issues with parking, accommodation, and overall crowd management.

6. **Sound restrictions:** Some hotels have sound restrictions, which can be problematic if you want to have loud music or a live band.

7. **Staff limitations:** Hotel staff may be limited in their ability to accommodate your needs, especially if they have other events happening at the same time.

8. **Space limitations:** Depending on the size of your wedding, a hotel may not have enough space to accommodate all of your guests comfortably.

9. **Time restrictions:** Some hotels have strict time restrictions on when events can start and end, which can be inconvenient if you want to party late into the night.

10. **Accessibility:** Hotels may not be easily accessible for guests who have mobility issues, which can create issues for some of your guests.

11. **Parking limitations:** Depending on the hotel's location, parking may be limited or expensive, which can be an issue for your guests.

12. **Lack of privacy:** Weddings in hotels may lack privacy, as there may be other guests, staff, or events happening at the same time.

13. **Limited catering options:** Some hotels have limited catering options, which can be problematic if you want to offer a unique or specialized menu.

14. **Restrictions on outside vendors:** Many hotels have strict policies on outside vendors, which can limit your ability to bring in your own vendors for photography, music, or other services.

15. **Competition with other events:** Hotels often host multiple events at the same time, which can create competition for resources and staff attention.

16. **Complexity:** Weddings in hotels can be complex and require a lot of coordination and planning, which can be overwhelming for some couples.

17. **Hidden costs:** Some hotels may have hidden costs, such as service fees or gratuities, which can add up quickly.

18. **Weather limitations:** If the hotel's outdoor spaces are an essential part of your wedding, weather limitations can be a significant drawback.

19. **Lack of flexibility:** Depending on the hotel, there may be limited flexibility in terms of the timeline, menu, or other wedding details.

20. **Poor communication:** Communication can be an issue when dealing with large hotels, especially if there are multiple points of contact and staff involved.

Most people do not realize that your event can get lost in a hotel due to multiple events going on at the same time, as there is a lack of any exclusive activity, and most ballrooms tend to be on the same floor level or even adjacent to each other.

Also, food quality and service tend to be poor, as most hotels are selling their name and not their food and service.

One of the biggest stressors is that most hotels do have adequate onsite parking for large gatherings, and valet services may be provided, but the time taken to get cars is usually long as vehicles need to be parked either on the road or in distant parking lots.

Another concern with hotels is that usually, they are not receptive to specific demands of guests, as banqueting is just one more income line in addition to the rooms and restaurants.

Food is usually not made specifically for the functions but is common to that served in buffets in restaurants and other functions, so there is no uniqueness to the menu.

C. Standalone Venues with Inhouse Catering and Decor

Apart from rental and hotel venues, there can be multiple other options of standalone venues with a mixture of these services and all other services you desire & deserve.

Pros:

- In such venues, you have one point of contact for the food, venue and décor, which is a huge saving of time and coordination.

- As all 3 key aspects are looked after by the venue, you usually get better value for money.

For such venues, these are their primary functions. Hence, they are most attuned to customer needs and usually ensure a far better quality of food, service and presentation.

These venues tend to be much more flexible with their menu and decor.

1. **Flexibility in terms of venue size:** Independent venues offer a wide range of venue sizes, so you can choose the one that best fits your guest list and budget.

2. **Unique atmosphere:** Independent venues often have distinctive architecture and interior design, which can add to the ambience of your wedding.

3. **Personalization:** You can customize every aspect of your wedding, from the décor to the menu, to fit your personal preferences.

4. **Privacy:** Independent venues offer greater privacy, as you don't have to share the space with other events.

5. **Competitive pricing:** Independent venues are likely to have lower pricing than hotels and resorts, which can help you save money.

6. **More options:** Independent venues offer more options for catering, bar service, and entertainment than traditional venues.

7. **Creative freedom:** You can let your creativity run wild when you host your wedding at an independent venue, as there are fewer restrictions and rules.

8. **Better parking:** Independent venues offer ample parking spaces available, which can make it easier for your guests to arrive and depart.

9. **Better accessibility:** Independent venues are generally located in convenient locations, with easy access to transportation.

10. **Reduced noise:** Independent venues are often located away from busy streets and highways, which can reduce outside noise during your wedding.

11. **More outdoor space:** Independent venues mostly have more outdoor space available for ceremonies and receptions.

12. **Technology Capabilities:** Independent venues have the latest technology, which can enhance your wedding experience.

13. **Lesser crowds:** Independent venues offer a more intimate setting with fewer crowds and distractions.

14. **Easier to create a theme:** Independent venues provide a blank slate for you to create your dream wedding theme.

15. **Better customer service:** Independent venues provide better customer service, as they have a dedicated staff that can focus totally on your event.

16. **More flexibility with timing:** Independent venues are more flexible with timing, allowing you to schedule your wedding at the time that works best for you.

17. **More natural light:** Independent venues often have more windows and natural light, which can enhance your wedding aesthetics & photos.

18. **Better acoustics:** Independent venues have better acoustics than traditional venues, which can improve the quality of your music and speeches.

19. **More personal attention:** Independent venues often offer more personal attention, as they are not as busy as traditional venues and can focus more on your event.

Cons:

- The venue could be at a distance from your hotel/residence.

- Transportation of guests to & from the venue could be additional.

- **If you do not select a genuinely professionally run venue, you could land up in deep trouble.**

Chapter 9

THE VENUE & DECOR CHECKLIST-
THE CORNERSTONE OF
A MEMORABLE WEDDING

After intensive observation, research and practical experimentation, I have developed this near-fail-proof checklist to help make the right venue & decor selection.

This will prove to be extremely useful to you, work through this checklist thoroughly without skipping any reference, and 70 % of your memorable wedding will be on track:

1. Check for the capacity of the Venue before finalization; is it compatible with your guest list?

2. Check for restrictions, specifically the time till which the DJ can play.

3. Power backup and load capacity?

4. Restrictions on guest numbers or any other factors?

5. Check the capacity of the onsite parking. Adequate onsite Parking is a must always to accommodate vehicles of your expected guests.

6. Check for any hidden costs or extra costs (Non-Exclusives-specifically question what is included and what is not). For example, the cost of Gensets, additional tables, chairs, waiters etc.

7. Check Extra Hours Fee: Does the venue charge extra for extra hours?

8. Check for the Alcohol Licence: Do you need to get an Alcohol Licence?

9. Check Corkage: Is it included in the Liquor prices, or does the Banquet permit you to buy liquor or pay corkage?

10. Check Catering: Is the Catering in-house, or will you have to arrange it separately?

11. **Check the Decoration:**

    a. Do they have an in-house Decorator, or will you have to arrange it separately?

    b. Check how open they are to customization.

    c. Check their portfolio of past Projects/Photos/Videos or orders and the themes they have created in the past.

d. Check if they have an in-house team for the flower work.

e. Do they provide specialized candles, fireworks, photo booths and other props etc.?

f. Ask whether they give references. If yes, check with those clients for feedback & reviews.

12. Check all hidden costs to arrive at an actual cost.

Leave Nothing to Chance: Do a Double-Check

To ensure that nothing is overlooked, the following list needs to be checked additionally:

g. Are there any additional charges?

h. Add what you like.

i. Delete what you do not like.

j. Thoroughly re-check what is included or excluded.

k. For what services and products are outside Vendors allowed?

13. How competent is the Manager?

14. Are the Promoters/Owners personally involved?

15. Are there additional backup Managers? (Is the team at Venue competent and capable?)

16. Is the Chef, who cooks food for sampling, the same one who will cook food for the whole function?

17. Are they willing to provide you with references?

19. How many Cuisines does the Venue make available?

20. Are they willing to provide you with the family tables?

21. Do they have the option of Brunch or Lunch?

22. Is it possible to get a part of the Menu specialized "GLUTEN FREE" or any other allergy-free?

23. Do they provide Jhatka or Halal choices?

24. To what extent can the decor be personalized?

25. Does the venue host single or multiple functions at the same time? A venue that hosts multiple functions is a CLEAR NO, as the personalized focus will be missing.

    Vendors doing multiple functions typically have diffused attention and will depute persons depending on the contract value which they may have signed with different hosts.

26. How responsive is the management to your requirements?

Most people opt for single-event hosting venues as the market in India is still fragmented and, at best, semi-professional.

Through the Stomach: Straight to the Heart

Food is perhaps the most fulfilling part of any festivity, and no matter how pleasing the decor, how wonderful the other arrangements are, if your food is not up-to-the-mark or rather beyond it— It will leave a bad taste literally :) pun intended.

Great food is a prerequisite for a memorable function. So here are some tips for curating an amazing and memorable menu:

A. It is strongly suggested that you opt for a Menu with in-house catering, as it saves time and money and frees you from heartburn and tension.

B. What is the ballpark figure of the venue? Does it fall within your expectations?

C. What are the inclusions and the exclusions in the Menu?

D. What type of food presentation do you want?

E. How elaborate do you want the menu to be?

F. What kind of an atmosphere are you creating for your event- Is the Menu aligned with that?

G. Do you trust the venue and the caterer? What is their reputation?

H. Do you want a tasting session- It is strongly recommended to have one.

I. When finalizing a menu, ensure it is made up of dishes which stand up on their own yet are in harmony with and complement the other dishes on the Menu.

J. Always try to take a multi-culture, multi-cuisine approach to the menu so that the entire mix of your guests will find something(s) to enjoy and cherish.

K. Ensure that the venue serves bite-size snacks and starters, as guests are usually holding a glass in one hand, talking, and interacting with other guests, and they must be able to get the snack in their mouth without struggling with a plate and a napkin.

L. Depending on your function size, ask for additional buffet tables to enhance the guest experience.

Memorable Wedding PROTIP 1

Always opt for Venues, which have inclusive catering, and provide tables, chairing and linen in their pricing, as this will save you a lot of costs and hassle.

Having an In-house decorator can take a lot of load off your shoulders & mind as they will themselves coordinate with the venues for Setup, Power-load etc., etc.

Now that you have evaluated your price, visit them, and prepare a list of questions which you will need to ask the venue.

There will always be variations in prices, terms, and conditions of all venues. Go with your gut and move forward with the venue where you and your guests will be cared for.

Understand and evaluate their terms and conditions. Are they transparent and fair? What is their cancellation policy?

Memorable Wedding PROTIP 2

All-inclusive event venues are usually able to get and give better deals from their vendors, the benefit of which passes on to the guests.

From a host's point of view, booking such venues will save you time and money and essentially make you tension free.

Memorable Wedding PROTIP 3

Never try to over-negotiate. Pushing any vendor beyond a point on pricing makes no sense as then they will be forced to cut corners & compromise on the services.

A good venue and good service providers save your time, effort, and money.

Any venue pushed too far beyond a point will simply lose interest, refuse a booking or just walk away.

If you want a good venue, caterer, decorator, singer or any professional to deliver as per your expectations, always respect their work and pay them their worth fairly.

Memorable Wedding PROTIP 4

Asking any professional or service provider to reduce their prices without offering them anything in return is an outright discount and will inevitably be resisted.

If you want to negotiate lower prices, offer them something of value in return.

- Maybe flexible payment terms.
- Maybe an additional booking.
- Maybe booking a smaller function as well.

So, dear readers, taking this journey forward, now the wedding dates are coming nearer. Based on the systematic tools that I have shared, you must now finalize the venue, caterer, decorator, photographer, videographer, DJ, performer, singer, or any other special requirements like a large display screen, pyrotechnics etc.

Chapter 10

SAVE THE DATE: SENDING INVITES

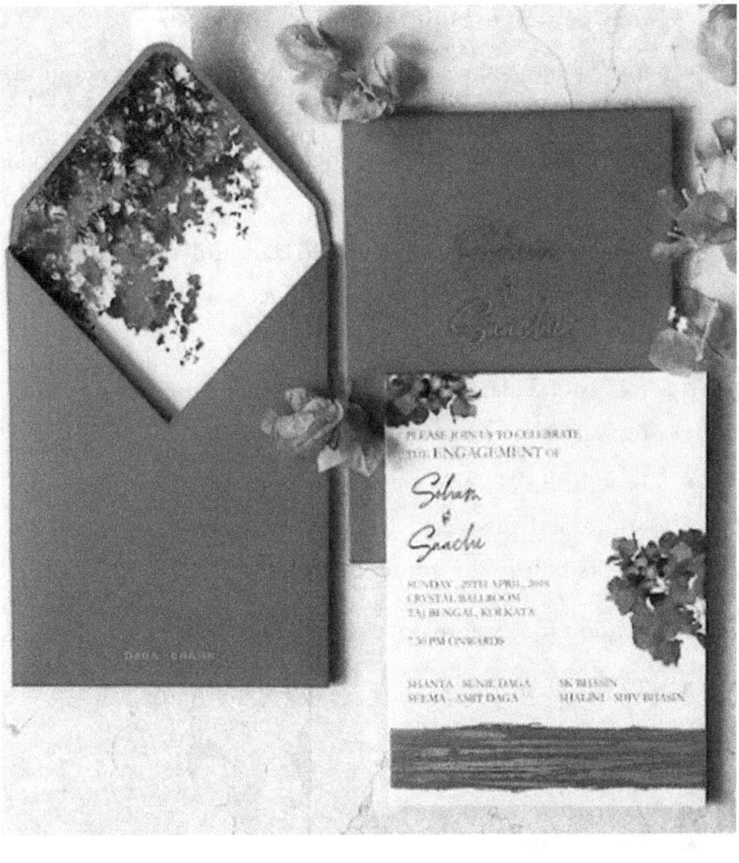

Once the venue and other arrangements have been finalized, now is the time to start sending out invitations.

This is how it is best to go about it

- Primarily, 6 to 9 months before the wedding date, a message should be sent out **specifying the date, the venue, and the City.**

- Secondly, 2 months before the wedding date, **invitations may be sent to confirm your guest count.**

- RSVPs should be sent **with multiple options to respond,** like Telephone No's, WhatsApp, Email and Form Links. (Your room bookings and other bookings will depend upon your guest count.)

- Always **designate a person to call and reconfirm** with guests who have responded and call to check with those guests who have not responded at all.

- It is a good idea to have an **RSVP Card Number** so that all responses can be **serially double-checked.**

- Post the RSVP cards with responses, **and attach a pre-self-addressed postcard. Request for responses at least 4 weeks before the actual deadline.**

It is a good idea to create an online site stating

- The location

- Time of function

- What to expect

- RSVP Link

Create and send login details to each guest individually.

For guests who confirm, provide them with the details of their hotel stay, transport arrangements, detailed programme, dress code and contact details of the facilitator/contact details of the designated person for general help.

Memorable Wedding PROTIP

Plan a timeline for all events, i.e.

When the function would start and when it is expected to end.

Also, outline the flow of events within the function. This will help things move smoothly and on time.

■ ■ ■ ■

ADDITIONAL MEMORABLE WEDDING PROTIPS

Here are additional 360-degree protips to ensure a memorable wedding.

- Delegate tasks & responsibilities to your friends and relatives who are responsible and willing to help. Alternatively, or additionally, hire one or two event coordinators who can assist you in managing the functions.

- Try to accommodate all your outstation guests in one location, maybe multiple hotels if one is not viable, but close to each other.

- Politely remind all your guests on the day of the function, the day before and 4/5 days before. Personalize your invite and personally ask about any special requirements they may have.

- Keep aside free time to welcome and meet your guests.

- Do not overload yourself with work related to the function, delegate and have a support team.

- Always limit your alcohol intake so that ceremonies are done on time, and everyone is fresh on the day of the function.

Cocktails and other such parties with alcohol should be hosted at least 24 hours prior to the wedding day.

- If providing travel options, provide dedicated vehicles for the guests, and share with your guests the contact numbers of the drivers; Alternately, keep a specialized Driver Coordinator whose duty would be arranging Pick and Drop facility for the Guests.

- Place a Welcome Kit and Basket in each room reserved for guests.

- Arrange for independent Ironing & laundry service.

- Create a packing list of clothes which guests should carry based on the season, location and theme/dress code of the event.

- Make a dedicated person in charge of specific functions, tasks.

- For your convenience, create a vendor list with names and contact numbers of persons, and alternate contact persons, names and contact numbers of the service providers.

- Create a timeline for the sequence of events.

- Create a DJ Playlist.

- Create a DJ Performer list if family members or guests are scheduled to join in.

- Work out an alcohol list.

- Always ensure with your vendor that they have a Back-Up Plan in place.

- Always keep your Vendors, Venue coordinators in the loop of any changes.

- Accept help from family and friends.

- Always be realistic. Do not aim for perfection.

- No matter what the issue, stay calm. The last thing anyone needs at a wedding is for someone, [especially the host(s)], to lose their cool. Slow down. Do not get hyper and over-reactive.

Go the Extra Mile

- Make your guests comfortable- inform your guests well in time as to what they should expect, travel times, dress codes, and the duration of the function.

- Don't spring any surprises on your guests- it doesn't always work out well. Always give them a heads up if they are expected to give speeches and live performances and share with them the programme schedule, distances of their hotels from the venue site, and distances from Landmarks to the venue.

- In case your guests are from other countries, please sensitize them to appropriate dress restrictions, local customs, and cultural behavior.

- Share with your guests a list of things to do in their free time, a list of specialities/tourist attractions of the region, suggested itineraries for sightseeing, and a list of specialist shops for buying local handicrafts, delicacies, and other takeaways.

The Cherry on the Top:
Memorable Post- Wedding Finishing Touches

A memorable wedding doesn't just end with the last ceremony and the departure of the guests. The flavor and fragrance of a memorable wedding linger post the wedding too. Not merely in the smiling faces of the joyous couple but in the last leg of care, courtesy and gratitude you extend to your invitees. After all, they made the occasion memorable with their participation.

Make sure to:

- Create and send creative-heartfelt thank you notes with thoughtfully chosen token gifts.

- These should be personalized and sent by letter or courier.

- Thank you notes must be sent to everyone who attended your functions, helped you in any manner in organizing the functions (including vendors & service providers), and those who have given any gifts or shown kindness in any manner, in any aspect of the organization of the event.

Hosting a **Memorable Wedding** is truly an **Art**. However, it is also something that everyone desires and deserves. With this book, I have shared with you in focused detail the blueprint for hosting a memorable wedding.

This art is no longer the domain of a lucky select few. I am sure if you follow some of the tips and take care of the identified major action points and follow the sequence and checklists religiously, you will have a really, really **Memorable Wedding** that you and your friends will cherish for a lifetime.

So go ahead and make that dream wedding a reality, completely stress-free........

So, how do we move forward with our/our child's dream wedding with no stress?

Now that you have read the book and reached here, I am sure that you are much more informed, more aware and have more clarity on how to go about curating a Memorable Wedding.....

The intention in writing this book was to empower and equip you with tools to curate a memorable wedding and take the stress out of organizing weddings and ensure that a wedding becomes a truly joyous occasion for your entire family as it should be.

I have deliberately kept the book compact so that everyone can read and implement it with ease and speed and enjoy the complete benefit of the information contained herein.

Dear Reader, after having read this book, you have two distinct choices:

Choice 1: You can absorb the suggestions in this book, get ideas from them and start implementing them yourself. And the result will undoubtedly be wonderful.

Choice 2: However, If you desire to go into greater detail, go deeper and ideate with someone who can almost guarantee you a stress-free, memorable wedding, someone who has vast and varied experience in organizing weddings and other functions, someone who can help you personalize and curate a really memorable wedding

with great value for money, then just email me at vikrantkuthiala@
vedasjammu.com and my team will arrange and fix a 1-2-1 Discovery
Call with me.

My promise: If I can help facilitate your dream wedding in any
way, I will be delighted to do so. No obligations!

As a gift, I have shared some sample wedding invitation letters for your ready reference, please modify them as required!

For Family & Relatives

Sample 1

Dear [Relative's Name],

Love is a beautiful journey, and we are thrilled to announce that our paths will forever intertwine as we embark on the journey of marriage. We invite you with open hearts and wide smiles to join us as we celebrate our wedding day.

The ceremony will take place on [Wedding Date] at [Wedding Venue], and we cannot imagine this day without your love and blessings. You have been a significant part of our lives, and your presence would make this occasion even more special.

Please save the date and make arrangements to be with us as we pledge our love to one another. We will be sending you a formal invitation with all the necessary details in due course.

Thank you for being a loving and supportive family member. Your presence will make our wedding day complete.

With love and anticipation,

[Your Names]

Sample 2

Dearest [Family Member's Name],

We hope this letter finds you in high spirits and good health. We are absolutely thrilled to share the news of our forthcoming wedding. It would be an honour for us to have you join us on this special day as we exchange vows and celebrate the beginning of a beautiful chapter in our lives.

On [Wedding Date], we will be gathering at [Wedding Venue] to celebrate our love and commitment. Your presence would make this day all the more memorable and joyous for us. We truly value the love and warmth that our family and relatives bring into our lives, and having you there would mean the world to us.

Please reserve this date on your calendar, and we will send you a formal invitation with further details soon. We eagerly await the day when we can share in the happiness and create lasting memories together.

Thank you for being a part of our lives and for your unwavering support.

We can't wait to celebrate with you!

Warmest regards,

[Your Names]

Sample 3

Dear [Relative's Name],

We hope this letter finds you in good health and happiness. We are overjoyed to announce that we have decided to join our lives together in the sacred bond of marriage. It is with immense pleasure that we invite you to be a part of our wedding celebrations.

On [Wedding Date], we will be exchanging vows at [Wedding Venue], surrounded by the love and blessings of our cherished family and relatives. Your presence on this auspicious day would make it even more special and memorable for us.

Please mark this date on your calendar and reserve the time to celebrate with us. We will be sending you a formal invitation shortly, which will provide you with all the necessary details.

Thank you for being a pillar of strength and love in our lives. We eagerly look forward to celebrating with you and creating beautiful memories that will last a lifetime.

With heartfelt gratitude,

[Your Names]

For Friends

Sample 1

Dear [Friend's Name],

It is with immense happiness that we invite you to be a part of our wedding day. Your friendship has brought us so much joy, and we can't imagine celebrating this special occasion without you.

The wedding ceremony and reception will take place on [Date] at [Venue]. We have planned an enchanting evening filled with love, laughter, and cherished moments. Your presence would make our celebration complete.

Please mark your calendars and kindly respond by [RSVP Date] to let us know if you'll be able to join us. We want to ensure that everything is arranged perfectly for you. If there are any accommodations or special requests you may have, please inform us in advance, and we'll do our best to accommodate them.

We genuinely hope you can be a part of our wedding day and share in the joy that fills our hearts. We look forward to creating beautiful memories together.

Warmest regards,

[Your Names]

Sample 2

Dearest [Friend's Name],

We are thrilled to extend our warmest invitation to our wedding day, and we would be honoured to have you join us as we exchange vows and embark on this incredible journey of love and togetherness.

The wedding will be held on [Date] at [Venue]. It will be an intimate affair, and your presence would make it even more meaningful. We have planned a delightful ceremony followed by a joyous reception to celebrate our union.

Please save the date, and we kindly request you to respond by [RSVP Date] so that we can make the necessary arrangements. If you have any preferences or requirements, please let us know, and we will ensure your comfort and enjoyment throughout the celebration.

We genuinely hope that you can share in the love and happiness that will fill the air on our wedding day. Your friendship is invaluable to us, and we can't wait to create beautiful memories together.

With love and gratitude,

[Your Names]

Sample 3

Dear [Friend's Name],

We are overjoyed to invite you to celebrate the most special day of our lives as we begin our journey together as husband and wife. You have been an integral part of our lives, and your presence would make our wedding day even more memorable.

The wedding ceremony will be held on [Date] at [Venue]. The festivities will commence with a heartfelt ceremony followed by a delightful reception filled with love, laughter, and music. We can't wait to have you share in our joyous celebration.

Please save the date, and we kindly request you to RSVP by [RSVP Date] so that we can make the necessary arrangements for your comfort. If you have any dietary restrictions or preferences, please let us know in advance.

We hope you can join us on this special day as we embark on a new chapter of our lives. Your presence means the world to us, and we look forward to celebrating with you.

With love and warm regards,

[Your Names]

I have also made some sample thank you letters that you can use as-is, or use them as inspiration to create your own.

Sample 1

Dear [Guest's Name],

We hope this message finds you in good health and happiness.

We are writing to express our sincerest appreciation for attending our wedding and sharing in the joyous celebration of our love and commitment.

Your presence on our special day meant more to us than words can express. It was a true honour to have you by our side as we embarked on this beautiful journey together. Your support and friendship have been invaluable, and we are grateful beyond measure for the love and warmth you have brought into our lives.

We also wanted to express our heartfelt gratitude for the thoughtful gift you gave us. Your generosity and thoughtfulness have touched our hearts deeply, and we are truly grateful for your kind gesture. The gift will be treasured as a symbol, a reminder of the love and support we have from friends and relatives.

Once again, please accept our sincerest thanks for being a part of our wedding day. Your presence and good wishes made the occasion all the more special. We are truly blessed to have you in our lives, and we look forward to the joy of creating lasting memories together.

With profound appreciation and warmest regards,

[Your Name] and [Spouse's Name]

Sample 2

Dear [Guest's Name],

We hope this letter finds you in excellent health and spirits. We are writing to express our utmost gratitude for joining us on our wedding day and making it an occasion to remember. Your presence and support meant the world to us, and we are deeply touched by your kindness and love.

We wanted to take this opportunity to extend our sincere thanks for the beautiful gift you gave us. Your thoughtful choice reflects your understanding of our tastes and desires, and we truly appreciate the effort and consideration you put into selecting it. It will hold a special place in our hearts and serve as a cherished memento of this joyous milestone in our lives.

Your warm congratulations and blessings have filled our hearts with joy and strengthened our commitment to one another. We feel blessed to have such amazing friends and family in our lives, and your presence at our wedding made it all the more extraordinary.

Thank you once again for your love, support, and generosity. We are forever grateful for your presence in our lives and for making our wedding day an occasion we will treasure always. We look forward to celebrating future milestones together and continuing to share in each other's joy.

With Heartfelt appreciation and warmest regards

[Your Names]

Sample 3

Dear [Guest's Name],

We hope this letter finds you in good health and high spirits. We both extend our sincerest gratitude for gracing us with your presence at our wedding ceremony. It was truly a day of love, joy, and cherished memories, and your presence added immeasurable warmth to the occasion.

We wanted to express our deepest appreciation for the thoughtful gift you presented to us. Your kindness and generosity touched our hearts, and we are truly grateful for your contribution to our new journey together. Your gift will serve as a constant reminder of this special day and the love we share.

It is the support of wonderful individuals like you that makes our journey as a married couple all the more meaningful.

Once again, thank you from the bottom of our hearts for making our wedding day truly unforgettable. We are incredibly blessed to have you in our lives, and we look forward to celebrating many more joyful moments together.

With warmest regards and deepest appreciation,

[Your Name] and [Spouse's Name]

I have also added an indicative checklist of all activities which need to be factored into a wedding, I am sure that this will help you keep things in focus!!

Indicative Checklist For Wedding Milestones

1. Finalize the wedding date.

2. Set a tentative budget for the wedding.

3. Create your first guest list.

4. Consult a wedding planner, if required.

5. Select a venue for all your functions.

6. Check and ensure a backup power source at all venues.

7. Plan and arrange for cocktails/reception and pre-wedding events like engagement, mehndi and sangeet.

8. Arrange for a pandit or religious officiant.

9. Finalize wedding rituals and specific family traditions to be followed with the pandit or officiant.

10. Select a caterer and menu for the wedding.

11. Decide on the wedding theme and décor.

12. Finalize the guest list for sending out wedding invitations.

13. Select and order wedding stationery (invitations, programs, menu cards etc.)

14. Hire a DJ or live music band for the reception.

15. Book performers or singers, if required.

16. Hire a wedding choreographer, if planning dance performances

17. Hire a wedding photographer and videographer.

18. Book a henna artist for the bride and guests.

19. Shop for bridal jewellery

20. Plan and order the groom's and bride's wedding attire.

21. Plan and take fitting trials for all clothes.

22. Arrange for wedding accessories like shoes, turban and sehra.

23. Book wedding night accommodation for the couple.

24. Book accommodation for out-of-town guests.

25. Organize accommodation and transportation for all guests who require it.

26. Apply for a marriage license and complete legal requirements.

27. Create a wedding day itinerary and timelines.

28. Arrange for wedding day refreshments and snacks.

29. Hire a Wedding day coordinator (If required).

30. Coordinate with the venue for parking arrangements.

31. Coordinate with the venue for any special requirements.

32. Arrange for wedding signage and directional boards.

33. Decide on the wedding cake design.

34. Confirm the wedding cake-cutting ceremony details

35. Organize a pre-wedding fitness and wellness routine.

36. Plan and book honeymoon travel and accommodations.

37. Prepare a list of must-have wedding photos.

38. Plan and book pre-wedding and family photo shoots.

39. Plan and book a post-wedding photo shoot.

40. Create a detailed shot list for the wedding photographer and videographer.

41. Finalize the ceremony music and song selections.

42. Confirm arrival times and schedules with all vendors.

43. Plan and book a pre-wedding spa day for relaxation.

44. Organize a pre-wedding medical check-up.

45. Arrange for backup transportation for the wedding day.

46. Prepare a wedding day emergency contact list.

47. Prepare a list of important phone numbers for the wedding day.

48. Create a detailed wedding day contact list for vendors.

49. Arrange for a wedding gift table and card box.

50. Arrange for steaming or pressing of all the clothes needed for the various functions.

51. Arrange for wedding day security at home, when the whole family is out for the wedding.

FINALLY

Relax, Enjoy Your Wedding Day & Celebrate!

Remember to customize this checklist based on your specific preferences, cultural traditions, and the scope of your wedding.

FUTURE WEDDING TRENDS!

Change is the only constant and the pace of change is ever increasing at a faster and faster pace, and weddings are no different. They are changing & evolving constantly too.

Keeping this in mind, I have highlighted a few of the impactful future trends to help you navigate the dynamic scenario with ease & joy.

1. **Ecology Driven Trends**

   Eco-friendly weddings: In alignment with the need of the hour to save the planet and battle climate change, more & more couples are choosing to opt for eco-conscious choices in terms of décor, invitations, and other wedding props etc.

   Sustainable fashion: Keeping with the leanings toward a safer and sustainable planet, there has already begun a shift towards sustainable and ethically sourced wedding attire, including organic fabrics and eco-friendly dyes.

   Zero-Waste Catering: To achieve sustainability goals for the planet & humanity, caterers will increasingly be forced to focus on zero-waste practices, such as composting food waste and using reusable serving ware.

Green Transportation: Since weddings entail a lot of guests which means more people using transportation, resulting in increased, sound & fuel pollution, Encouraging guests to carpool or use eco-friendly transportation options like electric vehicles is a great idea that is catching on fast.

Energy-efficient lighting: Energy is a critical area needing conservation, weddings and other public gatherings need to be careful about their energy usage. Utilizing LED lights or solar-powered lighting options to reduce energy consumption is the way to go.

2. **Technology-Driven Trends:**

Technology integration: With the advent of cutting-edge technology virtual reality, live streaming, and 360-degree video coverage will become more prevalent to enhance the wedding experience for guests who cannot attend physically.

Interactive wedding invitations: Technology is being used and will be used to create interactive digital invitations, incorporating videos, animations, and personalized messages.

AI-Powered Chatbots: Virtual assistants providing instant information and assistance for guests are likely to be a norm instead of a novelty soon.

Social Media Walls: Combining technology & social media, weddings will be made more interesting with displays showcasing real-time social media posts from the wedding.

3. **Socially Driven Trends:**

Intimate weddings: The trend of smaller, more intimate weddings that has taken the wedding world by storm of late will continue, with a focus on quality over quantity.

Multicultural weddings: As India becomes more diverse, intercultural weddings will rise, blending traditions from different regions.

Socially responsible weddings: A new and wonderful social trend on the rise is to leverage the visibility and connection of a wedding as a platform to support charitable causes and make a positive impact on society by setting new and socially responsible, sustainable trends. More and more couples are beginning to do this.

The wedding industry will continue to evolve and become more and more technology-driven, environmentally conscious and socially inclusive as we move forward, however, the heart of it all will still remain the emotions that make a wedding truly memorable.

So go ahead and make your/your children's wedding truly memorable with the secrets shared in this book......

■ ■ ■

QR for Feedback & **2 Free Gifts**

"The Wedding Budget Planner" &
"The Wedding Guest List Planner"